Embrace the Journey:

Navigating Autism with Love and Grace

by Tina Nicole

Table of Contents

Embrace the Journey: Navigating Autism with Love and Grace, First Edition

Published in 2025 by **Charles Jackson Media**

ISBN:979-8-218-77507-0
Library of Congress Control Number (LCCN): 2025918564

Subjects:

Parenting/Special Needs Parenting, Health & Family

Dedication

First and foremost, I give all honor and gratitude to God, whose blessings have guided and sustained me through every step of this journey. His grace has been my strength, and His wisdom my light.

To my incredible family, thank you for your unwavering encouragement, support and belief in me. Your love has been a pillar upon which I stand, and I am forever grateful for the ways you have lifted me.

To my dear godparents—your steadfast presence and boundless generosity have been a constant source of love and encouragement. Your support has extended not only to me but to my entire family, and for that, I am deeply grateful.

And to my amazing mother—your endless sacrifices, boundless love, and selfless devotion have shaped me in ways words cannot fully express. Your strength and grace have been my greatest example, and I am blessed beyond measure to be your child.

This book is a testament to the love, faith, and sacrifices that have brought me here. I love you all.

~ Tina

Part 1

It's ok

"Let the tears fall if they must; release makes room for resilience. But don't let sorrow linger—your child needs the strength only you can bring."

So...maybe you've noticed your child is a little different. Maybe a friend or family member put this book in your hands, hoping it would help. If you're reading this, I want you to know—you're not alone. I've sat right where you are, and I'm here to tell you: it's okay. It's okay to cry if you need to—sometimes, that release is what keeps us going. But don't let the tears linger all day; there's important work ahead, and your child needs you.

It's okay to feel a little angry or overwhelmed—those are real, honest feelings, and you're allowed to have them. Just try not to unpack and live there, because your health matters, too. Your family needs you, and together, we'll figure this out, one day at a time.

I went through my own emotional journey. I felt completely helpless. I couldn't understand why this was happening. I had done everything right: I ate nutritious foods, took top-quality prenatal vitamins, and stayed active throughout my pregnancy. When my child was born, there were no warning signs. He was a healthy 8 pounds 14 ounces, and the delivery was smooth and uncomplicated.

So, when he wasn't talking and his behavior didn't match that of other children his age, I was stunned. I felt fear, heartbreak, and even a bit of denial. But those feelings didn't define me. They fueled me. I became determined to understand, to advocate, and to move forward with purpose. I was DRIVEN. Driven to learn all I could.

I read books, looked online, and watched YouTube—anything to gain knowledge. All the research put me in overdrive, and I learned a lot. Most importantly, I trusted God, and you should too.

Trust that He has a plan for your children because He deeply loves them. We must be parents that God can trust. We are chosen and trusted by God to care for another life. It's an incredible opportunity and honor to be a parent.

It's okay if your child has special needs, or as I call them, **SUPER ABILITIES**! Learn their needs. If you've noticed differences, document them, ask questions, and find out what is typical for their age as a benchmark. Your child may be behind in some areas but ahead in others. Remember, it's not how you start the race, but how you finish.

Part 2

Signs

"Early signs don't define your child's limits; they invite you into deeper understanding." What feels overwhelming at first can become the doorway to clarity, connection, and a plan filled with hope."

*M*aybe your child isn't talking much, walks on tiptoes, spins at lights, or opens and closes cabinet doors repeatedly. I recall observing my child as he interacted with toys received for birthdays and Christmas. Unlike typical play patterns, his engagement was more exploratory in nature. Rather than using the toys in conventional ways, he appeared focused on examining their features—studying textures, shapes, or its mechanical functions.

This behavior should not be alarming. It reflects a sensory-driven or detail-oriented approach to playing, which is common among children on the autism spectrum.

Here are some indicators to help you evaluate your child's behavior and development. Early signs of autism spectrum disorder (ASD) in children can vary, but some common indicators include:

- **Social Communication Challenges (SCC):** Children with ASD may avoid eye contact, fail to respond to their name by 9 months, or not exhibit facial expressions such as happiness, sadness, or surprise by 9 months.

- **Delayed Language Skills:** They might not babble or coo by 12 months, say single words by 16 months, or use meaningful two-word phrases by 24 months.

- **Repetitive Behaviors:** This can include lining up toys, repeating words or phrases, and having obsessive interests.

- **Lack of Joint Attention:** They might not use their fingers to point in order to show interest in objects or events or engage in typical back-and-forth social interactions.

I understand this may be overwhelming. It was for me too. However, what feels overwhelming at first can become the doorway to clarity, connection, and a plan filled with hope. Let's create a plan.

Part 3

Pray and Plan

"My first step was prayer, and from that place of surrender came a plan. Thank God for the gift of your child, and ask Him for patience—because patience will become your greatest companion on this journey."

*A*ccepting a diagnosis for your child, in any capacity, is undoubtedly difficult to process. When I envisioned motherhood, I did not anticipate the possibility of having children with developmental delays. No one does. Though it caught me off guard, it never affected my love for my children. Love is alive!

A parent's love is an unbreakable bond of fierce protection, unwavering support, and endless devotion that transcends all boundaries.

When a child knows they are loved, they benefit in profound ways, including:

1. **Emotional Security:** Feeling loved provides a sense of safety and security, helping children to develop a strong emotional foundation.

2. **Self-Esteem:** Knowing they are loved boosts a child's self-confidence and self-worth.

3. **Resilience:** Love acts as a buffer against stress, enabling children to

better cope with challenges and setbacks.

4. **Healthy Relationships**: A loving environment, one that embraces differences, teaches children the importance of and how to form and maintain healthy relationships with others.

5. **Cognitive Development**: A stable, loving, peaceful, calm environment supports cognitive growth and the ability to learn and explore.

6. **Overall Well-Being:** Being loved contributes to a child's overall

physical and mental health, leading to happier and healthier lives.

My first step was to pray, and then I made a plan. I encourage you to do the same. Pray and thank God for your child. Then, pray for patience, as you will need it more than anything in my experience.

Here are a few scriptures that have helped me:

- **Galatians 5:22-23 (NIV):** But the fruit of the Spirit is love, joy, peace, forbearance, kindness, goodness, faithfulness, gentleness and self-control. Against such things there is no law.

- **James 1:3-4 (NIV):** Because you know that the testing of your faith produces perseverance. Let perseverance finish its work so that you may be mature and complete, not lacking anything.

Now, let's put our prayers into action and create a plan. Allow me to share an overview of the plan I used during the early years with my children. Your options and plan may vary depending on the type of medical insurance your child has.

1. **Consult with your Pediatrician:** Begin by consulting your pediatrician to review your child's benchmark scores.

2. **Request a Referral for a Pediatric Neurologist:** Ask your pediatrician for a referral to a specialist, specifically, a pediatric neurologist. A pediatric neurologist is a doctor who specializes in diagnosing and treating problems with the brain, spinal cord, muscles, and nerves in children — from newborns through young adults.

They handle conditions that affect how a child moves, learns, behaves, or develops.

This appointment may take some time to schedule and may not be local, but it is essential for obtaining comprehensive answers.

The neurologist's evaluation typically includes an in-depth neurological examination. This may include motor skills assessment, evaluation of reflexes, or electroencephalograph (EEG) test to identify abnormalities contributing to autism symptoms. The neurologist's prescription will supersede those of the pediatrician and counselors. This appointment, which can last over an hour, provides critical insights and hope by suggesting suitable career paths, such as architecture or radiologic technology.

3. **Arrange Extra Services:** There are additional support services that may be beneficial for your child. Your pediatric neurologist can provide the necessary prescription to initiate these services, which may include Behavioral Therapy, Speech and Language Therapy, Psychological Evaluation, or Occupational Therapy to name a few.

<u>It's important not to feel discouraged by the term "Behavioral Therapy</u>."

This type of intervention is not an indication of a behavioral problem. Rather, it can be a helpful tool in addressing habits such as finger-sucking and or repetitive behaviors, supporting your child's overall development in a positive and constructive way. Public schools typically offer these support services as part of their obligation to meet students' diverse educational needs. However, charter and private schools are not legally required to provide the same accommodations unless they are specifically structured to serve children with developmental or learning differences.

4. **Consult with School Guidance Counselors and Teachers:** Engage with your child's school guidance counselors and teachers, as your child may require an Individualized Education Plan (IEP).

Please understand, as you begin attending appointments, it's natural to wonder, *'How will I balance all of this with work?'* Take heart—you're not alone in that concern. After your child's diagnosis, one option worth exploring is

Social Security benefits, which may help lighten the load. Parents of children with disabilities may be eligible to receive Supplemental Security Income (SSI) through the Social Security Administration (SSA).

SSI provides monthly financial assistance to families with limited income and resources to help cover the costs of caring for a child with significant disabilities.

Eligibility Criteria:

To qualify for SSI benefits for a child, the following conditions must be met:

- **Age**: The child must be under 18 years old.
- **Disability**: The child must have a physical or mental condition that seriously limits their activities and is expected to last at least 12 months or result in death.
- **Income and Resources**: The family's income and assets must fall within the limits set by the SSA. These limits vary depending on household size and income sources.

Steps to Apply:

1. **Gather Documentation**
- Medical records, evaluations, and treatment history

- School records, including IEPs or 504 plans
- Proof of income and assets for the household

2. **Start the Application**
- Call the SSA at **1-800-772-1213** to begin the process
- Or visit your local Social Security office to schedule an appointment
- You can also start the **Child Disability Report** online at ssa.gov

3. **Complete the Interview**
- SSA will conduct an interview to assess eligibility
- Be prepared to discuss your child's daily functioning, medical

history, and how the disability affects their life

4. **Wait for a Decision**
- The SSA may take several months to review the application
- They may request additional evaluations or documentation during this time

Additional Support:

- **State Medicaid Programs**: If approved for SSI, your child may also qualify for Medicaid, which can help cover medical expenses.
- **Appeals Process**: If denied, you have the right to appeal. Many families succeed after providing

additional documentation or legal support.

Again, this amount of information may feel overwhelming. But get excited! You are on the right track. Regardless, take it one day at a time and one step at a time. This was my approach as well.

Additionally, I prayed for guidance and provision.

These are my **GO-TO** scriptures:

- **Philippians 4:19 (NIV):** And my God will meet all your needs according to the riches of his glory in Christ Jesus.

- **Matthew 6:31-33 (NIV):** So do not worry, saying, 'What shall we eat?' or

'What shall we drink?' or 'What shall we wear?' For the pagans run after all these things, and your heavenly Father knows that you need them. But seek first his kingdom and his righteousness, and all these things will be given to you as well.

- **Psalm 34:10 (NIV):** The lions may grow weak and hungry, but those who seek the Lord lack no good thing.

- **2 Corinthians 9:8 (NIV):** And God is able to bless you abundantly, so that in all things at all times, having all that you need, you will abound in every good work.

Each of these verses reminded me that God's resources never run dry. When I stopped stressing and started trusting, I saw His hand provide in ways I couldn't have imagined. He truly equips us for every good work He's called us to do.

Part 4

The Power of your Village

"God never intended for us to walk this road alone. Building your village of support is one of the greatest gifts you can give yourself and your child."

Building a Support Network

Navigating life with a child who has unique needs requires a strong, intentional support system. Over time, I've established three distinct "villages" that have been instrumental in our journey.

Family Village

My primary village is my family. My husband, mother, mother-in-law, and father-in-law have all played vital roles in supporting us. While no one is available all the time, it's important to be thoughtful about how and when you lean on this village. Their presence—whether emotional, physical, or logistical—can be a lifeline.

School Village

The second village is our school community, which includes teachers, speech therapists, counselors, and the principal. I made it a priority to schedule regular conferences—at least once per grading period—to stay informed about my child's progress, challenges, and achievements. These meetings were not always easy.

Hearing that my child was behind academically, struggling to read, or exhibiting disruptive behaviors in the classroom was emotionally taxing.

But I learned to take notes, ask for resources, and maintain my emotional balance. I reminded myself: *It's okay. We're learning and growing together.*

Sports Village

The third village is built through extracurricular activities, particularly sports. Depending on your child's physical abilities, explore options that suit their needs. My son doesn't have physical limitations, but he did need help with coordination. Team sports became a powerful tool—not just for physical development, but for social connection. Being part of a team gave him a sense of belonging and opened doors to friendships that extended into the classroom.

I'll never forget the moment he scored his first basket in a game. His teammates erupted with joy, running off the bench and cheering as if they'd won a championship. That moment brought tears to my eyes—it was more than a basket; it was a celebration of inclusion, effort, and love.

Additional Food for Thought

Introducing your child to swimming at an early age is highly recommended. It's a vital life-saving skill that every child should learn. Begin by helping them feel comfortable in the water - make it fun - gradually building their confidence and enjoyment during water activities.

If you live far from immediate family and don't have a village, consider looking into community programs that can enhance your child's development, such as sports, the arts, music, or animal shelters. Some of these programs specifically cater to children with special needs, helping them develop social skills.

Hearing another voice beside yours can greatly benefit them. Additionally, involving your children in extracurricular activities can provide you with a small break, allowing you to reset mentally and emotionally if needed.

Lastly, I strongly encourage you to take a parenting class. I did, and it was a tremendous blessing in my life. Although I love my children deeply, I had no prior experience with raising children with autism. One invaluable technique I learned is the Art of Redirection.

Instead of yelling "STOP!" When you want them to cease an activity, you gently redirect their attention. For example, if a child is scribbling on the walls, you could say, "Hey, let's draw on this paper instead! Look at all the fun colors we can use," while handing them a piece of paper and a crayon.

Simply redirect their interest in a more constructive and controllable manner.

Part 5

Ready for the Journey

"You are not walking this journey empty-handed—God has given you patience, provision, and a plan. As you move forward, you'll uncover unexpected strengths and discover hidden wonders within your child and yourself."

You're doing better than you think. The very fact that you've picked up this book is proof of how deeply you care—and that kind of love is what makes all the difference. Remember, you are loved, and God is providing you with patience and provision as promised in His Word.

You are well-equipped for this journey because you have a plan. Along the way, you will discover wonderful things about yourself, your support network, and your child. Through my experience, I found that nutrition was crucial. Here are a few changes I made that greatly impacted my kids.

1. **Removed gluten from my kids' diet. It significantly calmed them down.**

Here are a few more benefits:

- **Reduced Intestinal Inflammation:** For children with gluten sensitivities, removing gluten can help decrease gut inflammation and related symptoms, such as bloating, gas, and abdominal pain.
- **Improved Behavior:**

Some parents report improvements in their child's behavior, such as reduced hyperactivity and increased focus, after eliminating gluten from their child's diet. Food is fuel, but the wrong fuel can cloud the mind and agitate the body—while the right fuel can bring balance, clarity, and calm."

- **Increased Digestive Health:**

  A gluten-free diet can help alleviate digestive issues, leading to more regular bowel movements and overall better gut health.

- **Enhanced Nutritional Intake:**

By focusing on whole, natural foods, children may receive more essential nutrients, such as vitamins, minerals, and fiber.

2. **Eliminating artificial sugars and red color dye. It increased their focus at home and in school.**

Research has shown the following benefits of limiting sugar intake:

- **Improved Behavior:** Many parents report a reduction in hyperactivity, aggression, and tantrums after eliminating artificial dyes.

- **Better Focus and Concentration:** Children may experience improved concentration and focus on school and other activities.

- **Healthier Eating Habits:** Removing artificial dyes encourages a diet rich in whole, natural foods, which can lead to improved overall nutrition.

- **Reduced Allergic Reactions:** Some children may be sensitive or allergic to artificial dyes, and removing them can alleviate related symptoms.

- **Enhanced Well-being:** Overall, a diet free of artificial dyes can contribute to a child's physical and emotional well-being

3. **Enhancing their physical activity through sports, bike riding, outdoor games, and workouts—essentially anything that gets them sweating—can offer numerous benefits.**

Here are some key advantages of sweating:

- **Temperature Regulation:** Sweating helps cool the body, preventing overheating during physical activity.
- **Detoxification:** It helps eliminate toxins from the body, promoting a healthier internal environment.

- **Skin Health:** Sweating opens up pores and helps cleanse the skin, reducing the likelihood of skin issues.

- **Immune System Boost:** A routine of regular physical activity that induces sweating can strengthen the immune system.

- **Cardiovascular Health:**
  Activities that make kids sweat, like playing sports and other physical games, improve cardiovascular health by increasing heart rate and circulation.

- **Mood and Enhancement:**

Physical activity and sweating release endorphins, which can improve mood and reduce stress. These natural 'feel-good' chemicals act like the body's built-in reset button, helping to ease anxiety, sharpen focus, and boost overall emotional well-being.

- **Weight Management:**

Sweating through exercise helps maintain a healthy weight by burning calories.

I'll close with this. Your child's eating habits will play a crucial role, so be sure to consult your pediatrician regarding their nutritional needs. The right guidance can help you make small adjustments that lead to big changes in their energy, mood, and overall development.

Remember, nutrition is not about perfection—it's about creating a foundation that helps your child thrive.

Part 6

Choose Humor

"Sometimes laughter is the bridge that carries us through our fears. Humor doesn't dismiss the challenges—it lightens the load, opens the door for grace, and reminds us that joy is still part of the journey."

*I*t can be intimidating to allow your children to participate in activities with other kids, especially if you fear they might be bullied or picked on. I used to feel nervous at the playground because my children's speech was severely delayed, and I didn't want their challenges to be exposed. To manage my anxiety, I decided to approach the situation with humor.

When my kids, who were around 3 and 5 years old, would be asked by other children, "What did you say?" I would step in and say, "Hey sweetie, English isn't their first language." LOL! NEWSFLASH: English is our first language! (LMBO). The children and parents understood, especially since we lived in Miami, where many people spoke different languages. Sometimes, children or parents would ask what language my kids spoke, I'd jokingly say "Swahili"—a language no one around us actually spoke.

Living in Miami, I had to pick something obscure enough to avoid further questions, and to my surprise, they believed me! Later, I asked God for forgiveness, of course—but I laughed all the way home. My kids laughed with me, and honestly, it was the lighthearted moment I needed at the time.

Watching all the grandparents interact with their grandbabies was equally heartwarming for me. They tried so hard to understand them, but the delayed speech made communication challenging. After a trip to the mall, my son and his grandmother would return with a large shopping bag.

I'd ask, "Why did you buy so much?" She'd reply, "I couldn't tell which one he wanted, so I got them all!" We'd burst into laughter, and I'd tease, "We've got to figure this out soon—or we'll need

51

a loan!" Everyone gave them grace, and sometimes you must laugh to keep going.

Keep moving forward. Wake up each day with intention—parent with purpose and grace. This is the beginning of a beautiful journey. Embrace it fully, learn from each moment, and allow it to shape you. As you overcome challenges, your story will inspire and uplift other parents walking similar paths.

Your life is a book—make it a bestseller!

YOU GOT THIS!!!

May God bless you and your family. May His peace and protection surround you always. From our family to yours, we send our love.

~ Tina

About the Author

Tina Nicole is a devoted mother of four, track coach, writer, mentor, community organizer, and successful entrepreneur. With a vibrant blend of experience, leadership, education and compassion, she has dedicated her life to empowering others—especially families and young people—to thrive with purpose and faith. Her own journey of discovering God as a teenager fuels her passion to help students and parents alike embrace their calling, overcome challenges, and walk confidently in who they were created to be.

Through her work as a coach, mentor, and community leader, Tina has inspired countless lives with her unwavering belief that love and grace can transform even the most difficult seasons. When she's not writing, coaching, or organizing community initiatives, Tina enjoys building her businesses, staying active in sports, and sharing laughter through family games and competitions.

Her life is a beautiful testament to resilience, faith, and the joy of living fully in every role God has entrusted her with.